Lifelines 4

Josiah Wedgwood

An illustrated life of Josiah Wedgwood

1730-1795

Richard Tames

D0308558

Shire Publications Ltd

CONTENTS

ACKNOWLEDGEMENTS

The author wishes to thank Josiah Wedgwood and Sons Limited, Barlaston, Stoke-on-Trent, for permission to reproduce all the illustrations save that on page 15 (upper), and is especially grateful to Mr William A. Billington, former Curator of the Wedgwood Museum, Barlaston, for his invaluable assistance. He also wishes to acknowledge Mrs T. B. Jarvis (Hon. Sec., the Wedgwood Society) for her assistance, and the Morley Hewitt-Jarvis Collection for the photograph on page 15 (upper).

The publishers acknowledge the kind assistance of Miss Gaye Blake Roberts, Curator of the Wedgwood Museum, Barlaston, in preparing this second edition.

The cover picture is a portrait of Josiah Wedgwood by George Stubbs and is reproduced by courtesy of the Trustees of the Wedgwood Museum, Barlaston, Stoke-on-Trent, Staffordshire, England.

Printed in Great Britain by C. I. Thomas & Sons (Haverfordwest) Ltd, Press Buildings, Merlins Bridge, Haverfordwest, Dyfed.

Left, Josiah Wedgwood FRS, 1730–95, from the portrait by Sir Joshua Reynolds.

The Churchyard House and Works, Burslem, where Josiah Wedgwood was born.

EARLY LIFE 1730–1765

Boyhood and youth

Josiah Wedgwood was born at Burslem in Staffordshire in 1730, the last of a family of twelve, the fourth generation of a dynasty of potters. Having started school at the age of six, he was 'a fair arithmetician and master of a capital hand' at nine, when his father's early death obliged him to leave school. At fourteen, until he was nineteen, he commenced an apprenticeship to learn 'the Art, Mistery, Occupation, or Imployment of Throwing and Handleing' but this was impeded by an abscess which frequently made him unable to use the throwing wheel. Enforced leisure, however, gave him the opportunity for study and he used his time well to gain a thorough grounding in the scientific knowledge of his day.

In 1754 Wedgwood entered into a partnership with Thomas Whieldon, a highly successful local manufacturer who encouraged him to experiment and introduce improvements in manufacture. His reputation must already have been considerable, for the terms of agreement were very generous — any discoveries made by Wedgwood were to be used for the benefit of both partners, but the actual secrets of manufacture were to remain Josiah's exclusive property. By 1759 sufficient capital had been accumulated for Josiah to set up on his own. His first premises, the Ivy House and Potworks in Burslem, were rented from his uncles at £15 a year and consisted of a cottage, two kilns, some sheds and extensive workshops on two storeys.

Wedgwood soon showed that he was his own most expert employee, already a master of the technical aspects of his trade and beginning to show a flair for management in a wider sense. He prepared his own mixtures of clays, designed the wares and supervised the firings. He made a good product and he knew how to make it efficiently and sell it with style.

The prospects for pottery

Superficially the outlook for a young master-potter was far from promising. The local industry was primitive and without reputation and the country was so isolated by the badness of its roads that it seemed it would never be possible to break out into a wider market. Conditions were, however, changing as steam-power, turnpike roads and canals made their gradual impact on industry and commerce. More important, from the 1740s onwards the population of Britain, which had been near-static for half a century, began to expand with increasing rapidity, extending, as never before, the markets open to men of enter-prise. For these growing numbers plate was too expensive, pewter too scarce, porcelain too fragile. The way was open for the tough, cheap, durable earthenware pot. Changing tastes were also favourable. Polite society drank coffee and chocolate and, by mid-century, nearly everyone was drinking tea. In 1757 Jonas Hanway's famous *Essay on Tea* put forward a vigorous criticism of the new fashion as certain to lead to national decline. England, he argued, was already rich in beverages—'We have abundance of milk; beer of many kinds; lime which we import from countries in Europe near at hand; infusions of many salutary and well-tasted herbs; preparations of barley and oats; and above all, in most places, exceedingly good water.' Tea, Hanway alleged, was ruining to both the constitution and the character. It impoverished the poor and gave rise to a great con-traband trade. 'When it is genuine', he claimed, 'it hurts many, when adulterated or dyed, it has been found poisonous . . . What a deplorable situation is that poor creature in, who having but three pence or a groat a day, consumes a quarter part or more of her income in the infusion of a drug which is but a remove from poison.' The fashion had spread with alarming rapidity—'The young and old, the healthy and infirm, the superlatively rich, down to vagabonds and beggars, drink this enchanting beverage, when they are thirsty and when they are not thirsty'. Heedless of Hanway's exhortations to 'follow the dictates of their own common sense' and 'disdain such a servility to custom' the British made a fashion into a custom, the custom into part of their way of life and a prop to their national character.

The century was remarkable also for the growing prosperity it brought to all classes. In 1779 the guests of the Rector of Aston 'sat down to table, which was covered with salmon at top, fennel sauce to it, melted butter, lemon pickle and soy; at the bottom a loin of veal roasted, on the one side kidney beans, on the other peas, and in the middle a hot pigeon pie with yolks of eggs in it. To the kidney beans and peas succeeded ham and chicken and when everything was removed came a currant

6

The new creamware

The Brick House Works, Burslem, known as the Bell Works because the workmen were summoned by ringing a bell instead of by blowing a horn as was the custom.

tart . . .' Rising incomes and susceptibility to the dictates of the fashions of London and Bath meant a general refinement of taste among the middling ranks of society and in their new standards of domestic comfort lay great market opportunities for the Lancashire weaver, the Sheffield cutler and the Staffordshire potter. Josiah Wedgwood was by no means slow to appreciate the position which confronted him. As he wrote in the introduction to his *Experiment Book* — 'I saw the field was spacious, and the soil so good as to promise ample recompense to any who should labour diligently in its cultivation'.

In 1759 he commenced his own business at The Ivy House Works but the premises soon became too cramped and the business shifted to the larger Brick House Works. Josiah had a bell hung to summon the men to work and this innovation led to the pottery's re-christening as the Bell Works.

The new creamware

Wedgwood's most important product at this time was a cream coloured earthenware, much improved as a result of his experiments. The ingredients of this were Cornish china clay,

THOMAS BENTLEY.
1730—1780. Modelled
by Joachim Smith, 1774.

china stone, ground flint and Devon ball clay. It was then covered with a tough lead glaze and the result was in Wedgwood's words, 'a species of earthenware for the table quite new in its appearance, covered with a rich and brilliant glaze bearing sudden alterations of heat and cold, manufactured with ease and expedition, and consequently cheap, having every requisite for the purpose intended'. This new ware was the foundation of Wedgwood's success, and killed the general manufacture of delft, with its softer tin-enamel. Versatility was the outstanding quality of this new product which could be thrown on the wheel, turned on a lathe or cast and lent itself to the new, simple lines of the neo-classical style, which was unsuitable for both delft and porcelain. The great porcelain factories at Meissen and Sevres, the subsidized creations of royal patronage, gradually began to give way before the products of a purely commercial enterprise from a distant province of a nation which had formerly been content to import its fine wares and imitate where it could not import. Looking back from the vantage point of 1829, George Robertson wrote: 'among all the improvements made in the household furniture and utensilry, the greatest about this time was the introduction of a new species of dishes from England, instead of the old, clumsy, Dutch delft-ware, and the more ancient pewter plates . . . In the course of a very few years it spread over the whole country; and being fully as cheap as any . . . was very readily adopted in the farmers' families, as it displaced none of their own handyworks, and was highly agreeable to the females of the house'.

Bentley, business and marriage

In 1762 a leg injury obliged Wedgwood to remain for several tedious weeks in Liverpool, where his doctor introduced him to Thomas Bentley, a local merchant. Bentley had travelled widely in Europe, and his excellent education at Findern Academy, Derbyshire, and his thorough training in business methods had brought him to a position of some eminence in Liverpool, where he had helped to found the Nonconformist Academy, the Public Library and the Octagon Chapel. Pleasing in manner and appearance and with a wide knowledge of scientific, literary and artistic matters, he struck up an immediate friendship with Wedgwood which soon blossomed into a business arrangement.

Wedgwood also had attained some social prominence by this time. In 1763 he was chosen by his fellow potters to act as their advocate before Parliament in promoting a new local turnpike and it is probable that he helped to draw up the official petition, which, incidentally, tells us that:

'In Burslem and its neighbourhoods are nearly 150 separate potteries for making various kinds of stone and earthenware, which, together, find constant employment and support for nearly 7,000 people. The ware in these Potteries is exported in vast quantities from London, Bristol, Liverpool, Hull and other seaports to our several colonies in America and the West Indies, as well as to every port in Europe'.

In the same year Wedgwood made new standards of craftsmanship and design attainable by the introduction of 'engine-turning'. Recent French modifications of the simple lathe, principally the invention of a cutting-tool which could be moved longitudinally by a screw-thread, enabled the operator to pare away clay, to reduce thickness and to cut precise circles which defined form more clearly. Fluting and beading, based on ancient designs wrought in metal, could now be reproduced easily, as well as the more complex squared and 'diced' patterns which were produced later on. Wedgwood had heard of engine-turning being used in metal-work at Aston Hall, near Birmingham, and he was extremely proud of having seen the potential of this machine-tool for the pottery industry.

In 1764 Wedgwood married a distant cousin, Sarah Wedgwood, and a year later their first child, Susannah, Josiah's beloved 'Sukey', was born.

The origin of the use of flint in pottery
'The use of Flint in our Pottery is said to have proceeded from an accident happening to one of our Potters, a Mr. Heath of Shelton, on his way to London. His Horses eyes becoming bad, he applied to an Horsler on the Road, who told him he could cure the Horse, and would shew him what means he used. Accordingly he took a piece of black Flint Stone, and put it into the fire, which to our Potter's great astonishment came out of the fire a most beautiful white . . . He brought some of the stones home with him, mixed them with Pipe Clay, and made the first White Flint Stone Ware.'

from Wedgwood's writings

THE ESTABLISHMENT OF ETRURIA 1765–1775

The first canals

Master of a thriving business, master of a growing household, Wedgwood was now to take on a new responsibility. In March 1765 he wrote to his brother:

'On Friday last I dined with Mr. Brindley, the Duke of Bridgewater's engineer, after which we had a meeting at the Leopard on the subject of a Navigation from Hull, or Wilden Ferry, to Burslem agreeable to a survey plan being taken. Our Gentlemen seem very warm in setting this matter on foot again, and I could scarcely withstand the pressing solicitations I had from all present to undertake a journey or two for that purpose.'

Wedgwood's local standing and his experience on turnpike trusts naturally thrust him to the fore in this venture, but he needed no convincing of the value of canals. The cost of transporting bulky raw materials and fragile finished products had to be included in the final selling price of every article. Cheaper and more regular transport meant an even flow of production, fewer breakages, lower prices, wider markets and greater sales. Wedgwood became an active promoter of the scheme for a 'Grand Trunk' Canal, connecting the Potteries with Hull and Liverpool. The efforts of Wedgwood and his fellows in winning over local support, raising money, distributing pamphlets and organizing meetings and petitions led finally to the successful passing in May 1766 of an Act of Parliament which authorized the construction of a canal to unite the rivers Trent and Mersey and in June Wedgwood was elected treasurer of the project. He ceremonially cut the first sod in July. The section from the Trent to the Potteries was completed in 1772, but the canal, which was 93 miles long, was not completed until 1777, owing to the difficulty of constructing the 2,897 yard long tunnel at Harecastle, one of the engineering wonders of the age. The total cost of the venture was estimated at £300,000.

Potter to Her Majesty

In 1765 Wedgwood received an unexpected, and quite unsolicited, order to make a tea service for Queen Charlotte. Swift to realize the commercial value of this stroke of fortune

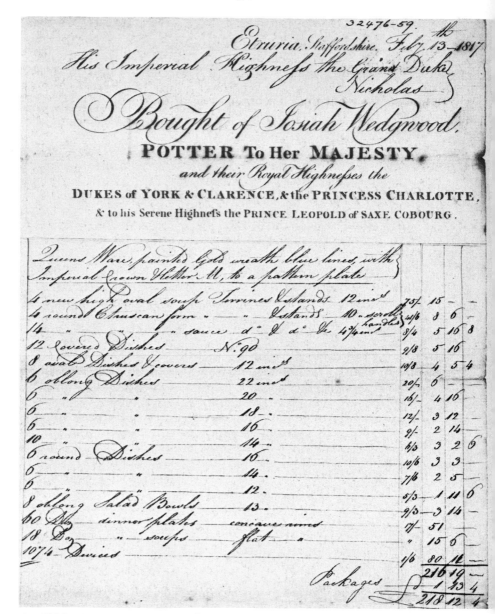

An 1817 bill for a crested Queen's Ware service.

he wrote to his brother in London: 'Pray put on *the best suit of Cloaths you ever had in your life* and take the first opportunity of going to Court.' Samples and patterns were sent for the Queen's approval, as a result of which Wedgwood was able to record, 'To this manufacturer the Queen was pleased to give her name and patronage, commanding it to be called Queensware, and honouring the inventor by appointing him Her Majesty's Potter.'

The execution of the work required very difficult gilding, but Wedgwood took it as a challenge and succeeded himself in making powdered gold (usually pounded in honey which was later washed away) at the first attempt, which pleased him greatly, because 'I have always been told one man only in England could make it'. Added to technical problems were labour troubles and he complained that 'I am just teazed of my life with dilatory, drunken, idle, worthless workmen which prevents my proceeding in the tea service, to which more sorts of workmen are necessary than one would imagine.' Nevertheless royal patronage was a valuable commercial asset and from 1767 onwards 'Potter to Her Majesty' began to appear on the Wedgwood bill-heads and the firm's London show-rooms were later known as The Queen's Arms.

Wedgwood could now sell his common earthenware under the prestigious title of Queensware and was soon able to write triumphantly—and perceptively—'the demand for this Cream-colour, alias Queensware . . . still increases. It is really amazing how rapidly the use of it has spread over the whole Globe, and how universally it is liked. How much of this general use, and estimation, is owing to the mode of its introduction—and how much to its real utility and beauty? are questions in which we may be a good deal interested for the government of our future Conduct.' He drew the moral for himself—'if a Royal, or Noble introduction be as necessary to the sale of an article of Luxury, as real Elegance and beauty, then the Manufacturer, if he consults his own interest will bestow as much pains, and expense too, if necessary, in gaining the former of these advantages, as he would in bestowing the latter.'

The search for patronage and publicity

Wedgwood realized that if he could woo and win the patronage of the influential few, he could count on the custom of the masses who followed their example. After the Queen came the Princess Dowager and their Royal Highnesses the Duke of York and Albany and the Duke of Clarence. Methodically Wedgwood followed the maxim he had formulated — 'begin at the Head first, and then proceed to the inferior members'. In his efforts to please the leaders of fashion and taste he undertook many special commissions which were, in themselves, unprofitable and, as 'Uniques', incapable of being mass-produced. Nevertheless they were invaluable in winning 'warm Patrons' and as a form of exclusive advertisement for the technical skill and artistic flair of the Wedgwood manufactory. With Bentley's diplomatic skill to aid him Wedgwood soon created a clique of aristocratic admirers whose casual gossip was the highest recommendation a fashionable product might aspire to. Thus Wedgwood advises his London partner to 'preview' a new range of bas-relief vases — 'Sir William Hambleton [Sir William Hamilton, Ambassador to Naples, who was largely responsible for making known the classic art unearthed at Herculaneum] our very good friend is in town — Suppose you shew him some of the vases and a few other Conoisseurs, not only to have their advice, but to have the advantage of their puffing them off against the next Spring, as they will, by being consulted, and flatter'd agreeably, as you know how, consider themselves as a sort of parties in the affair, and act accordingly.' Nor was the fair sex neglected, because Wedgwood knew that 'few ladies . . . dare venture at anything out of the common stile till authoris'd by their betters — by the ladies of superior spirit who set the fashion'. Fashionable artists and architects of the day were similarly consulted — Romney, Stubbs and Joseph Wright of Derby used Wedgwood vases as background ornaments for their paintings; the brothers Adam and 'Capability' Brown were all targets of Josiah's solicitations in the grand strategy to build up 'lines, channels and connections' in the fashion-conscious society of eighteenth century England. As Forster, a contemporary writer, put it, 'In England the several ranks of men slide into each other almost imperceptibly . . . Hence arises a strong emulation in all the several stations and conditions to vie with each other; and a perpetual restless ambition in each of the inferior ranks to raise themselves to the level of those immediately above them. In such a state as this fashion must have an uncontrolled sway. And a fashionable luxury must spread through it like a contagion.'

Classic designs

Condiment cruet in Queen's Creamware (1780–85).

Part of a page from an early catalogue for Wedgwood Queen's Ware.

A CATALOGUE,

Of the different Articles of QUEEN's WARE, which may be had either plain, gilt, or embellished with enamel Paintings, manufactured by JOSIAH WEDGWOOD, Potter to her MAJESTY.

A SERVICE of QUEEN's WARE, of a middling Size, with the lowest *wholesale Price*, at Etruria, in Staffordshire.

						s.	d.		£.	s.	d.
	2 Oval Dishes,	—	19 Inches	—	—	2	6	—	0	5	0
	2 Ditto	—	17	—	—	1	6	—	0	3	0
	2 Round Dishes	—	17	—	—	1	6	—	0	3	0
	2 Ditto	—	15	—	—	1	0	—	0	2	0
	4 Oval Dishes	—	15	—	—	1	0	—	0	4	0
	4 Ditto	—	13	—	—	0	8	—	0	2	8
	4 Ditto	—	11	—	—	0	5	—	0	1	8
	4 Round Dishes	—	11	—	—	0	5	—	0	1	8
	4 Covered Dishes	—	—	—	—	2	0	—	0	8	0
*Fig. 3, 24, 27.	2 Terrines for Soup	—	—	—	—	7	0	—	0	14	0
Fig. 13.	2 Sauce Terrines	—	—	—	—	2	0	—	0	4	0
Fig. 10, 11, 12.	4 Sauce Boats	—	—	—	—	0	5	—	0	1	8
Fig. 25.	2 Salad Dishes	—	—	—	—	1	4	—	0	2	8
Fig. 6 & 33.	6 Salts	—	—	—	—	0	4	—	0	2	0
	2 Mustard Pots	—	—	—	—	0	4	—	0	0	8
	4 Pickle Dishes	—	—	—	—	0	3	—	0	1	0
	6 Dozen flat Plates	—	—	—	—	2	6	—	0	15	0
	2 Dozen Soup ditto	—	—	—	—	2	6	—	0	5	0

This Service plain, No.   comes to   —   —   —   2 17 0

Classic designs

Even before he had received royal approbation Wedgwood had begun looking for a site for a new factory. In December 1767 he bought Ridge House Estate, 350 acres lying between Hanley, Burslem and Newcastle. The projected factory, which was to specialize in the production of 'ornamental' rather than 'useful' ware, was named Etruria, a tribute to the universal, and mistaken belief that the Greek and Italian pottery newly discovered at the excavations around Pompeii was Etruscan in origin. After 1773 the Etruria factory became less specialized, and 'useful' as well as 'ornamental' wares were made there.

The taste for extravagant baroque and rococo designs was fading—profuse decoration, vivid colours and heavy gilding were now all beyond the pale, and the new demand was for the antique, the pure, the simple, now seen in the original by growing numbers of milords on the 'Grand Tour'. Wedgwood was swift to satisfy the taste for the neo-classical and based his vases on the urns and amphorae of the ancients, decorating them with delicate garlands and fine fluting. He reproduced ancient cameos and even revived the lost art of encaustic painting. He knew that his products must accord with the prejudices of his age, however, and bade Flaxman design decorous draperies for athletes, warriors and nymphs, warning him that to cover 'the nudities . . . with leaves . . . is not enough—for none either male

Below left; a modern replica of a Jasper portrait medallion, white on blue, of Captain James Cook.
Below right; a modern reproduction portrait medallion of John Wesley.

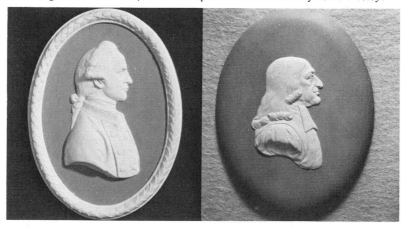

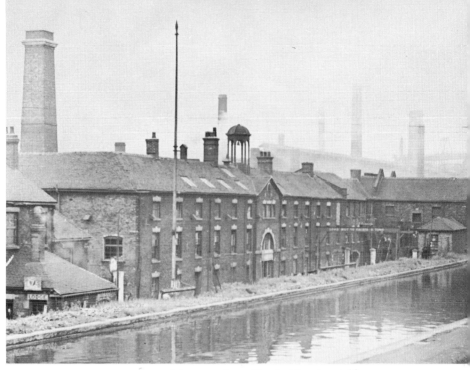

A view of the former Wedgwood factory alongside the Trent and Mersey canal at Etruria.

or female, of the present generation, will take or apply them as furniture if the figures are naked'.

Contemporary souvenirs

Contemporary events also had commercial potential and as early as 1766 Wedgwood wrote to Bentley—'What do you think of sending Mr. Pitt upon Crockery ware to America? A Quantity might certainly be sold there now and some advantage made of the American prejudice in favour of that great Man'. When Admiral Keppel was tried by court martial in 1779 and, to the joy of the populace, acquitted, Wedgwood wrote at once, begging for a picture to copy and regretting that for once he had been slow off the mark. 'Oh Keppel, Keppel—Why will not you send me a Keppel. I am perswaded if we had our wits about us as we ought to have had two or three months since we might have sold £1,000 worth of this gentleman's head in various ways, and I am perswaded it would still be worth while to disperse them every way in our power.' In time Wesley, Garrick, Dr. Johnson, Joseph Priestley, Mrs. Siddons and Captain Cook were all acclaimed in cameos, buttons, rings, seals and bracelets, while popes were made for export to Italy and Spain, saints for South America and Mohammed for Turkey.

Bentley and Wedgwood

While Etruria was under construction Wedgwood was trying to wheedle Bentley away from Liverpool to join him in a full partnership.

'Can you exchange the frequent opportunities of seeing and conversing with your learned and ingenious friends, which your present situation affords you, besides 10,000 other elegancies and enjoyments of a Town life, to employ your self amongst Mechanics, dirt and smoke . . . ? . . . if you think you could fall in love with, and make a Mistress of this new business, as I have done of mine, I should have little or no doubt of our success . . . we have certainly the fairest prospect of enlarging this branch of Manufacture to our wishes, and as Genius will not be wanting I am firmly persuaded that our profits will be in proportion to our application . . .'

Wedgwood valued Bentley's taste and sent him a copy of D'Hancarville's recently published *Antiquites, Etrusques, Greques et Romaines* bidding him choose examples of vases and other pottery which might be suitable for reproduction. The letter which accompanied the book contained the interesting request that Bentley should take his sister's advice before making any final selection, for, Wedgwood claimed:

'I speak from experience in Female taste, without which I should have made but a poor figure amongst my Potts, not one of which of any consequence, is finished without the Approbation of my Sally.'

Troubles with smallpox

In 1767 inoculation of infants against smallpox was first advocated and Wedgwood, who had suffered disablement from that terrible disease, submitted his two-year-old daughter and one-year-old son to the new practice. He later confided to Bentley that:

'They both had Convulsions at the first appearance of the eruption, and have had *a pretty smart pox* as our Doctor terms it. I believe they have had no dangerous symptoms, but have been so very ill and I confess I repented what we had done, and I much question whether we should have courage to repeat the experiment, if we had any more subjects for it . . .'

The smallpox soon had a terrible revenge. Wedgwood's right leg, which had always been troublesome, incapacitated him

Josiah Wedgwood and his family in the grounds of Etruria Hall, by George Stubbs. This picture, painted in 1780, now hangs in the Wedgwood Museum at Barlaston.

entirely in May 1768 and his doctors decided that it must be amputated. Drugged with laudanum, he survived the operation but on the very day Wedgwood's bandages were removed for the first time, his year-old son Richard died.

Etruria

Building at Etruria proceeded slowly, delayed by rain and difficulties with the architect, Pickford, who submitted a new estimate, double the original one, half way through the course of construction. The internal layout of the factory was strongly influenced by that of Matthew Boulton's Soho ironworks outside Birmingham, opened in 1766. Boulton, 'the complete manufacturer in metal' and partner, patron and counsellor of

James Watt, became one of Wedgwood's most important associates, mounting and setting in bronze the products of Etruria. When the scheme was first mooted there were doubts in the Wedgwood camp but Josiah made a shrewd assessment of of the situation in a letter to Bentley:

'Mr. Boulton and I go a-curiosity hunting all day tomorrow . . . What do you think of it? Perhaps you would rather he would let them alone. Very true, but he will be doing, so that the question is whether we shall refuse having anything to do with him, and thereby affront him, and set him of doing them himself . . . If we join with him in this scheme, I apprehend we can always bind him to us by making him such things as nobody else can, and thereby make it his interest to be good. We can make things for mounting with great facility and dispatch and mounting will enhance their value greatly in the eye of the purchaser . . .'

On 13th June 1769 Etruria was ceremonially opened by Wedgwood and Bentley with a pot-making ceremony in which six copies of a black Etruscan vase were thrown by Wedgwood, while Bentley turned the wheel. Hand-painted on one side with three figures from Sir William Hamilton's *Etruscan Antiquities* and the words *Artes Etruriae Renascuntur* (the arts of the Etruscans are re-born); on the other side they bore the legend

June XIII MDCC LXIX

One of the first Day's Productions

at

Etruria in Staffordshire

by

Wedgwood and Bentley

Despite this act of ceremonial co-operation it was soon decided that Bentley should reside in London, not at Burslem, and take care of the sales and distribution of Wedgwood's sought-after wares.

Sales techniques

Even from a distance of 200 miles Wedgwood continued to bombard his partner with ingenious plans for promoting his wares. He disapproved of a plan to distribute handbills as being beneath the dignity of a manufacturer patronised by the highest in the kingdom. 'We have hitherto appeared in a very different light to common shopkeepers, but this step (in my opinion) will sink us exceedingly.' Instead he pressed on with advertisements in the fashionable news-sheets, solicited 'puffing' articles from influential critics and extended the use of his trade mark to cover more of his range of products. He was not above suggesting that they should circulate rumours that some of their finest products might become scarce.

'This idea will give limits, a boundary to the quantity which your customers will be ready to conceive may be made of these bas-reliefs, which otherwise would be gems indeed. They want nothing but age and scarcity to make them worth any price you

One of the six Black Basalt 'First Days' vases which were made to commemorate the opening of the Wedgwood factory at Etruria.

could ask for them.' Wedgwood does not seem to have been altogether happy about this idea, however, as he asked Bentley to burn the letter in which he put it forward. A more successful and imaginative idea was the satisfaction-guaranteed-or-your-money-back policy which Wedgwood was the first manufacturer ever to introduce. He also paid the cost of carriage on all goods to London, and later extended it to part payment of carriage to any place in the kingdom. In his showrooms he held 'ticket only' displays of new goods for the 'Nobility and Gentry', had pattern books available for ladies to skim through while awaiting entry and even altered his prices to conform with notions of taste—'I think', he wrote to Bentley, 'what you charge 34/- should . . . be . . . a Guinea and a half, 34 is so odd a sum there is no paying it Genteely'. Self-service facilities were introduced and special attention was paid to display. Vases were put out in ones and twos to give an impression of rarity. 'Every new show, Exhibition or rarity soon grows stale in London, and is no longer regarded after the first sight,' Wedgwood observed, 'unless utility, or some such variety as I have hinted at continues to recommend it to their notice . . . I have done something of the sort since I came to Town and find the immediate good effects of it. The first two days after the alteration we sold three complete sets of vases at two and three guineas a sett, besides many pairs of them, which Vases had been in my Rooms 6—8 and some of them 12 months and wanted nothing but arrangement to sell them.'

Ambassadors and export agents

Bentley was by no means a mere agent and used his charm and tact to make numerous important contacts in diplomatic circles and he took to heart Wedgwood's admonition that 'every Gentle and Decent push should be made to have our things seen and sold at Foreign Markets. If we drop or do not hit of such opportunities ourselves we cannot expect other People to be so attentive to them and our trade will decline and wither, or flourish and expand itself, in proportion as these little turns and opportunitys are neglected or made the most of.' Via ambassadors, envoys and consuls Wedgwood ware entered the courts of Russia, Poland, Spain, Portugal, Denmark, Sweden, the Netherlands, Turkey, Naples and Turin. A thousand parcels, containing £20,000 worth of pottery, were dispatched to the minor nobility of Europe in an attempt to imitate the domestic strategy of starting at the top of the social pyramid and proceeding downwards. This, in turn, was followed by the production of special lines for each mass-market—intricate decoration for France, where the rococo still prevailed; 'shewy, tawdry, cheap things, cover'd all over with colors' for Russia; cheap goods and 'seconds' for America and special exotic designs for Turkey. Gradually the great European factories, Sevres, Meissen, Vienna and Paris, began to imitate his designs and Stanislas Augustus, King of Poland, 'wishing to put an end to

the considerable loss in currency caused by purchases of table-
ware manufactured in England' subsidized the establishment of
a royal pottery in the grounds of his palace.

Using the peerage

When he heard that 'there seemed to be a violent *vase madness*
breaking out' in Ireland, Wedgwood scribbled hasty instructions
to Bentley, 'This disorder should be cherished in some way or
other, or our rivals may step in before us. We have many Irish
friends who are both able and willing to recommend us . . . Lord
Bessboro' you know can do a great deal for us with his friends
on the other side of the Water by a letter of recommendation or
otherwise as he may think proper. You are to visit him soon—
the rest will occur to you . . . We are looking over the English
Peerage to find out *lines, channels and connections*—will you
look over the Irish Peerage with the same view—I need not tell
you how much will depend upon a *proper* and *noble* introduction. This, with a fine assortment of Vases and a Trusty
and adequate Agent will ensure us success in the conquest of
our sister kingdom.'

The prospect of foreign sales was never, however, allowed to
detract from giving due attention to the domestic market and
Bentley received similar strings of instructions for this purpose:

'. . . deliver cards at the houses of the Nobility and Gentry and
in the City . . . have an Auction . . . Make a great route of
advertising this auction, and at the same time mention our rooms
in Newport Street and have another Auction in the full season
at Bath or such things as we have now on hand just *sprinkled
over* with a few new articles to give them an air of novelty . . .
and a few modest puffs in the Papers from some of our friends.'

A time of troubles

The years 1770–1772 were difficult and Wedgwood proved
his worth as a businessman by learning how to prosper in
adversity. Bentley's talents did not extend to efficient super-
vision of the London staff. Dishonest clerks embezzled funds
and the rest let the paper-work slide into chaos and the debts
into arrears. All that Bentley could do was to constantly in-
voke Wedgwood's name, until Josiah was moved to protest that,
'My name has been made such a Scarecrow to them that the
poor fellows are frightened out of their wits when they hear of
Mr. Wedgwood's coming to town.'

There was more than inefficient clerks to worry about, however: Wedgwood's father-in-law became ill, which deprived him

23

Josiah Wedgwood

temporarily of the support and company of the wife upon whom he depended so heavily; he began to suffer from eye-strain; a rival circulated the malicious rumour that he had 'run away for no less a sum than £10,000!' He feared that he might lose his sight altogether, 'I am often practising to *see* with my fingers, and think I should make a tolerable proficient in that science for one who begins his studys so late in life, but shall make a wretched walker in the dark with a single leg.' In February 1770 he wrote to Bentley, asking him to come to Burslem to learn all he could about pottery, 'I am sensible of my danger, and the last attack may be sudden and not give me an opportunity of communicating many things which I would not have to die with me.'

Fortunately Wedgwood's eyes improved and he was able to devote himself to pulling the business out of the disastrous depression which threatened to engulf the whole trade.

The London rooms had nearly £5,000 of stock on hand, instead of the usual £1,000 worth, and at Burslem, Wedgwood was struggling to pay his workmen and his running debts simultaneously. Lady Cathcart, the wife of the British Ambassador in St. Petersburg, came to the rescue with orders from Russia. Wedgwood saw that 'this Russian trade comes very opportunely for the useful ware, and may prevent me lowering the prices here . . . the General trade seems to me to be going to ruin on the gallop—large stocks on hand both in London and the country, and little demand. The Potters seem sensible of their situation, and are quite in a Pannick, and indeed I think with great reason, for *low prices* must beget a *low quality* in the manufacture, which will beget *contempt*, which will beget neglect and disuse, and there is an end of the trade. But if any one Warehouse, distinguished from the rest, will continue to keep up the quality of the Manufacture, or improve it, that House may perhaps *keep up its prices* and the *general evil* will work a particular good to that house, and they may continue to sell *Queensware at the usual prices*, when the rest of the trade can scarcely give it away. This seems to be all the chance we have, and we must double our diligence here to give it effect.'

Threat of a strike

In 1772 Wedgwood was faced with the threat of a strike at Etruria.

'This morning all the Men at the Ornamental work were assembled to meet me at half past six, on the outside of the Gates, in order to expostulate with me about their prices . . . I then talked to them altogether about quarter of an hour and after producing several instances of their extravagant charges I told them we would *make a new sett of hands*, which they must be sensible was in my power to do, rather than to submit to give such prices as must in the end ruin the Manufacture, both to us, to themselves, and their Children after them . . .' The men went back to work and Wedgwood, absorbed now with the problems of selling rather than of producing, began to aim at the 'Middling Class of people', rather than the 'Great People'. His new strategy was to produce ornamental ware by mass production techniques. He had unwittingly made a start in this direction by building up a supply of moulds so that semi-skilled workers rather than master potters could turn out saleable articles, 'to make such machines of men as cannot err'.

Josiah Wedgwood

Mechanization and increased productivity

The wage disputes of 1772 prompted him to examine in detail the cost structure of his business. His analysis led him to see the point of the workmen's complaint that they wasted valuable time 'tuning their fiddle' to make only limited quantities of an article. In addition to this he came to realize the importance of overheads, like the cost of the buildings, which remained fixed however much or little was produced. The solution was to make 'the greatest quantity possible in a given time', spreading the fixed costs over a larger number of articles, whose price could be proportionately lowered. Greater mechanization would enable him to increase output while lowering price rates, and increased productivity kept the men's wages steady. The result would be a breakthrough into a new mass market—'The Great People have had these Vases in their Palaces long enough for them to be seen and admired by the Middling Class of People, which Class we know are vastly ... infinitely superior, in number to the Great, and though a great price was, I believe, at first necessary to make the Vases esteemed Ornament for Palaces, that reason no longer exists. Their character is established and the middling People would probably buy quantitys of them at a reduced price.'

The Frog Service

The years 1773-74 were taken up with the execution of a spectacular commission from Catherine the Great of Russia for a table and dessert service of 952 items of ware. Intended for use in the palace of La Grenouilliere the service was to bear the emblem of a frog and each piece was to be decorated with a different view of England. The cost in plain creamware was a mere £52. The enamelling, however, kept Wedgwood's Chelsea works occupied for a year and, when it was displayed in the new London showrooms in Greek Street, Soho, the 952-piece service was adorned with 1,244 views. Wedgwood realized the immense publicity value of this, the greatest of all his 'Uniques'. A really stunning display would, he assured Bentley, 'bring an immence number of People of Fashion into our Rooms—Would fully complete our notoriety to the whole Island, and help us greatly, no doubt, in the sale of our goods, both usefull and ornamental— It would confirm the consequence we have attain'd, and increase it, by shewing that we are employ'd in a much higher scale than other Manufacturers. We should shew that we have paid many compliments to our Friends and Customers and thereby rivet them the more firmly to our interests . . .'

The Frog Service

Some of the trial pieces made by Josiah Wedgwood for the 'Frog Service' for Empress Catherine of Russia. Left; a compotier, hand-painted in enamel but without the frog crest, depicting Stoke Gifford, Avon. Below; the compotier with three dinner plates, two of which display the frog crest.

The show, in new rooms in Greek Street, Soho, was visited by Queen Charlotte, Prince Ernest of Mecklenburg, and the King and Queen of Sweden. For over a month the nobility and gentry followed in their footsteps while the common folk gawped at the lines of carriages outside. The choice of subject alone assured success for the exhibition, for almost all of those whose country seats were represented on the service trekked up from the shires to see them. Some trial pieces of the service were also made but without the Frog and these were displayed at Etruria and possibly at Greek Street. Wedgwood's worst fear which he had confided to Bentley when the original order was received–'Suppose the Empress should die when the service is nearly completed'–was not confirmed. The Empress Catherine paid 16,406 roubles and 43 kopecks (about £2,700) for the service but the profit was very small for, although the actual cost is not known, Josiah's estimate of the cost of production was £2,410.10.5. The financial gain may have been small but the prestige and publicity gained from this stupendous venture was enormous.

The invention of Jasper

Wedgwood issued his first catalogue of ornamental ware in 1773, of the Queensware range in 1774. Absorbed in experiments to find suitable materials to manufacture a true 'English' stoneware, he paused to discuss with Mr. Samuel More, the secretary of the Society of Arts, the possibility of starting a definitive and complete collection of 'Wedgwood and Bentley' for posterity. 'I have often wished', Wedgwood confessed, 'I had saved a single specimen of all the new articles I have made . . . For 10 years past I have omitted doing this, because I did not begin it ten years sooner . . .'

The experiments came to fruition in 1774 with the invention of Jasper. Cornish clay was used in the making of his Jasper wares which are a type of vitrified 'stoneware' although when such things as cups were made very thinly they had a slight translucency. It was impervious to water, did not need glazing and could be cut and polished on a wheel. Any shade of blue could be attained and 'likewise a beautiful Sea Green'. Experiments to improve the new composition continued for several years but were hampered by the need to obtain raw materials without inadvertently revealing the secret to rival manufacturers.

The search for Jasper had been inspired by the desire to imitate Roman cameo glass, like the famous 'Portland' vase.

3435 *Continued*

of 22 to 1605 would not prevent its staining upon a coloured ground, which 1605 & 2688 or F white, were very liable to do, and it has answered that purpose in a great measure, for it is much less liable to take a stain by being laid upon a colored ground than either of the other bodies, and is very proper for small gems for rings. It likewise preserves the sharpness & bears a variation in burning, better than either 1605 or 2688.

3435 + has 3000 of 22 ground fine, & is used for cameos Nov. 10. 178
The grounds are 3435, & the colored washes for the grounds from the same ——

3436 Sept.r 1779. Tried $-\frac{10}{10}$ & $\frac{}{5}$ Say 3436 +

3437 This is to harden the Jasper, and make it proper for seals.
It answers very well ——

3438
3440 These three Nos. are for the white of the small cameos upon dark ground, and the fired & ground 2688 or F white is added to prevent cracking; for as they should be ground finer than the grounds need to be, they would from that circumstance shrink more than them in the burning if the fired composition was not added — the F white has not that effect — it is found to have the effect of flint, which is fluxing

3441 Black wash for the above white = is the same as 2807 +
3442 Blue for Nicola, or black & blue onyx = ... 3443
3443 For grounds for the above colours = ... 3430 } only
these 3441, 3442, & 3443, have for their basis one & the same No. viz. 3435, that they may all be of one nature, & shrink alike in burning, and not warp & crack, as they will when three or four colours are used in the same piece, & each colored clay is of a different composition.

3444 &c. — N.B. — 1, 2, 3, &c. are different specimens of 15.

Reproduced from Josiah Wedgwood's experiment book, part of his code to various raw materials used in thousands of trials for new bodies, glazes and colours.

Opaque coloured glass, usually dark blue, was dipped into white molten glass, which was subsequently cut away to leave white designs on a coloured ground. More subtle effects could be obtained by varying the thickness and number of layers of glass. This type of work could be done equally well in Jasper, which was the most important innovation in ceramics for very many years. On Bentley's recommendation Wedgwood employed John Flaxman, the brilliant young sculptor, to execute neo-classical designs for a new range of Jasper wares.

THE YEARS OF ENLIGHTENMENT 1775–1795

Business as usual

The years 1775-1779 were relatively uneventful. Experiments continued as usual; the London employees continued as inefficient as usual; minor lawsuits over patents, new designs for vases and cameos, and public affairs, particularly the war in America, occupied Wedgwood's attention. William Hackwood, an 'ingenious boy' hired in 1769, developed into a skilful modeller of portraits and figures in bas-relief. Wedgwood complained that he was 'growing very extravagant in his prices and I do not find it possible to keep him reasonable upon that subject' though he was well pleased with the work. Portrait cameos became an important part of the Wedgwood range in later years, but Josiah had a swifter success with new pestles and mortars, produced by his own process, 'a new excellent composition and cheap'. With characteristic flair he arranged for them to be launched at Apothecary's Hall and publicly proved 'with the severest necessary tests'. In June 1779 the Greek Street showrooms were honoured by another Royal visit. In thanking Bentley for his account of the occasion Wedgwood remarked perceptively — 'Fashion is infinitely superior to merit in many respects; and it is plain from a 1,000 instances that if you have a favourite child you wish the public to fondle and take notice of, you have only to make choice of proper sponsors. If you are lucky in them no matter what the brat is, black, brown or fair, its fortune is made!'

In November 1780 Bentley died. Wedgwood was severely shaken by the loss of the man who had been his partner and intimate friend for more than 17 years. For friendship he turned more and more to the poet and scientist Erasmus Darwin, grandfather of famous naturalist, and long the Wedgwood family's consultant physician; in the business Wedgwood came to rely on his nephew, Thomas Byerley, a former actor, teacher and writer, who having tried his hand in New York, London and elsewhere, had returned to Burslem to become a mainstay of the family firm.

Fellow of the Royal Society

Wedgwood, now past his fiftieth year, busied himself with further scientific experiments. As a personal friend of Joseph Priestley, the eminent chemist, he often attended the monthly meetings of the Lunar Society, which met at the time of the full moon. Nor was he a mere amateur in scientific matters. In 1783 he succeeded in inventing a pyrometer, a thermometer capable of measuring very high temperatures, which became a part of ceramic industry equipment for the next 20 years. In recognition of the value of his invention he was elected a Fellow of the Royal Society early in 1783.

The same year saw the end of the American War of Independence. Wedgwood's sympathies throughout had been with the colonists and the blunderings of the British government filled him with indignation—'Somebody should be made to say distinctly what has been the object of the present most wicked and preposterous war with our brethren and best friends . . . I am glad that America is free and rejoice most sincerely that it is so, and the pleasing idea of a refuge being provided for those who choose rather to flee from than to submit to the iron hand of tyranny raises much hilarity in my mind.' His immediate concern, however, was to represent the interests of the Staffordshire

An eighteenth century specimen of Josiah's pyrometer and descriptive pamphlet.

potters before the House of Commons while a commercial treaty was being negotiated.

Corn riots

During his absence in London a food riot took place at Etruria. A succession of two bad harvests had driven the local price of wheat up to an unusually high level and when it was rumoured that a barge load of corn was being taken to Manchester to be sold at inflated prices, a mob seized the barge and sold the corn at what they considered a 'fair' price. It took several days for the local gentry to mobilize the militia and disperse the mob but the arrest and trial of two of the ringleaders ended the matter.

As a result of the riots Wedgwood composed *An Address to the Young Inhabitants of the Pottery* warning them not to be misled by the violence of their elders and to remember instead that they were fortunate to live in a growing and prosperous area. 'I would request you to ask your parents for a description of the country we inhabit when we first knew it; and they will tell you that the inhabitants bore all the marks of poverty to a much greater degree than they do now. Their houses were miserable huts, the lands poorly cultivated . . . and these disadvantages, with roads almost impassable, might be said to have cut off our part of the country from the rest of the world . . . Compare this picture, which I know to be a true one, with the present state of the same country, the workmen earning near double their former wages, their houses mostly new and comfortable and the lands, roads and every other circumstances bearing evident marks of the most pleasing and rapid improvements . . . Industry has been the parent of this happy change'— and Wedgwood had himself been almost the sole creator of that industry.

The prudent employer

Another pamphlet of 1783 was one entitled *An Address to the Workmen in the Pottery on the Subject of Entering into the service of Foreign Manufacturers* which bore on the title page the warning 'A rolling stone gathers no moss'. Wedgwood did not fear imitation; indeed he welcomed it as a tribute to his standards of design and workmanship — 'So far from being afraid of other people getting our patterns, we should glory in it, throw out all the hints we can, and if possible have all the artists in Europe working after our models. This would be noble, and would suit both our dispositions and sentiments much better than all the narrow mercenary selfish trammels'. The idea of generally uplifting popular taste appealed to Wedgwood, but he did fear that his competitors might steal, not his designs or his skilled workmen, but knowledge of the secret compositions and manufacturing techniques which were the real foundation of his success. Prudence, as well as humanity, therefore prompted him to treat his workmen in an enlightened and liberal manner. Following Boulton's example at Soho he set up a sick club at Etruria and contributed generously to the cost of establishing schools in the district.

The General Chamber of Manufacturers

Wedgwood himself was now taking a leading role in formulating national commercial policy. In 1771 he had promoted meetings of local potters to maintain prices; in 1772 he recommended that the association of potters at Hanley should subsidize experiments which would be of general benefit to the trade. Informal meetings in later years discussed matters of common concern, like prices, restrictive patents and foreign tariffs. The negotiation of an Irish Trade Treaty in 1785 offered the opportunity, in Wedgwood's opinion, to establish a General Chamber of Manufacturers which would be both national and permanent in its organisation, co-ordinating the efforts and representing the interests of the many existing local associations, clubs, meetings and chambers of commerce. Several of Wedgwood's associates—notably Boulton and his friend Samuel Garbett—joined him in his efforts to give the temporary alliance of manufacturers a general and permanent character, but their interests were too divergent and their enthusiasm too spasmodic for any enduring institution to emerge.

Industrial espionage

Industrial espionage for instance was becoming a major problem and Wedgwood hoped that the General Chamber might take effective action against 'foreign spies' of whose activities he had been informed by 'Mr. Watt and some other Birmingham gentlemen'. Writing to William Nicholson, Secretary of the General Chamber, Wedgwood advised placing advertisements in the newspapers to warn manufacturers of the devious ploys that might be used against them—'having been refused admittance by one clerk, they have come again when he was absent, and almost forced their way to the machines they wanted to see. In another instance, having been turned out of one door, they have waited an opportunity of entering in under different pretences by another. Sometimes they pretend to be possessed of improvements to the machines they want to take drawings or models of. At other times they procure recommendations from gentlemen who are not aware of their intentions, or even bring the gentlemen themselves with them, when they can prevail upon them so far, and in short use every possible means to accomplish the purposes they are come hither for and therefore no time should be lost, nor any vigilance spared on our part to prevent them.'

Emigration and intercepted letters

Emigration continued to worry Wedgwood more than his contemporaries in other trades, who depended less on secret processes and more on the simple excellence of their production, management and marketing. Wedgwood's pamphlet had warned workmen that if they were seduced into the service of a foreign master they might easily be cast aside when they had given away all they knew. There was mounting evidence to suggest however that the initiative sometimes came from the workmen themselves. The following letter was addressed to George Bris of Douai, in Belgium:

'. . . I understand you want some workman in the Different Branches of the potting and I have it in my power to serve you if we can agree upon terms. I can bring a turner, a presser and handler, a modeller and a man that can make as good a China glaze and Enamel colours as any man in the country and both he and me are painters either in blue or enamel, likewise his wife . . . if you chuse I will come my self first and settle for one of us and come back a gain to England for them . . . All the rest of us are married except my self and I will run the hazard of any thing happening from the masters in this country. You must excuse my not dating my letter . . . for I do fear it should be broken open . . .' It was, and presumably joined a file of intercepted correspondence on the subject of emigration.

The negotiation of a new commercial treaty with the French offered a further opportunity for strengthening the General Chamber. Wedgwood was encouraged by Eden, the chief negotiator of the treaty, but Pitt, the Prime Minister, was opposed to aiding any association which might at some date limit his political freedom of manoeuvre. The ratification of the treaty proved to be the cause of the final wrecking of the General Chamber. When it was brought before Parliament for its approval the aggressive and confident manufacturers of the North and

Midlands welcomed it as a step towards free trade and a stimulus to exports; their colleagues in older industries which had not benefited from the new steam technology, feared the competition of imports, passed resolutions against the treaty and petitioned Parliament to withhold ratification. Wedgwood took a philosophical consolation from the situation and with characteristic largeness of vision wrote–'An exchange of the produce of one nation for the manufactures of another are happy circumstances, and bid fair to make the intercourse lasting; but sensible as I am to the interests of trade, manufacturers and commerce, they all give place to a consideration much superior in my mind to them all. I mean the probability that a friendly intercourse with so near and valuable a neighbour, may keep us in peace with her—may help to do away with prejudices as foolish as they are deeply rooted, and may totally eradicate that most sottish and wicked idea of our being natural enemies . . .'

The Slave Trade

The demise of the General Chamber left Wedgwood free to concentrate his energies on a new cause — The Society for the Suppression of the Slave Trade, founded in 1787. He became a member of the Committee and was now as active in promoting petitions, distributing pamphlets and persuading the influential for the cause of abolition as he had been 20 years before in promoting turnpikes and canals. Clarkson, the historian of the abolition movement, recorded how influential in gaining popular support was the cameo which Hackwood modelled and Wedgwood produced, showing a kneeling slave, manacled and begging, with the inscription 'Am I not a man and a brother?' Hundreds of the cameos were produced and, according to Clarkson, 'At length the taste for wearing them became general and thus fashion . . . was seen for once in the honourable office of promoting the cause of justice, humanity and freedom'. In 1789 Wedgwood produced another commemorative medallion in honour of the founding of the first British colony in Australia, at Sydney Cove, New South Wales. The clay from which the medallion was made was sent from Sydney Cove itself and Wedgwood declared it was 'an excellent material for pottery and may certainly be made the basis of valuable manufacture for our infant colony'. The medallion showed Hope addressing Peace, Art and Labour, and inspired Erasmus Darwin to compose a lengthy speech for Hope, which Wedgwood charmingly acknowledged as '. . . the

This medallion, by William Hackwood, chief modeller at Etruria from 1769 to 1832, and depicted as the seal of the Slave Emancipation Society was first struck in 1786 by Josiah Wedgwood to help William Wilberforce in his campaign for the abolition of slavery. It was produced again in 1959, the firm's bicentenary year, to commemorate the 200th anniversary of Wilberforce's birth.

prettiest lines I have read a long time . . . and so apropos that I cannot but wish to have it made longer by the same hand'. In the same year Wedgwood also produced a medallion to celebrate King George III's restoration to sanity.

Retirement

1789 was, of course, the year of the French Revolution. Wedgwood greeted its moderate beginnings with as much enthusiasm as any other liberal Englishman. In a letter to Dr. Darwin he affirmed, 'I know you will rejoice with me in the glorious revolution which has taken place in France. The politicians tell me that as a manufacturer I shall be ruined if France has her liberty, but I am willing to take my chance in that respect, nor do I yet see that the happiness of one nation includes in it the misery of its next neighbour. A gentleman who is just come from his travels has been here a day or two, and he assures me that the same spirit of liberty is developing itself all over Germany, and all over Europe.'

In 1790 Wedgwood reached his sixtieth year and began to turn over the management of his business to his sons and his nephew, Tom Byerley. Wedgwood's eldest son, John, had received an excellent education at the Academy that Bentley had helped to found, had spent a year in Edinburgh and had been sent on two tours of the Continent. The second, which took him to Rome for a year, was intended to combine business with learning but served only to strengthen John's resolve not to join the family firm full-time, 'as I should thereby lose a great part of the advantage of the liberal education I have received'. This came as no surprise to his father, who had predicted in 1779 that his education, which was mainly classical, would spoil him for business. John's younger brothers, Josiah and Tom, had received much of their more practical and scientific education at Etruria and it was upon them and the invaluable Tom Byerley that much of the daily management and research work now devolved.

The Portland Vase

Wedgwood senior, therefore, was free to devote all his energies to the masterpiece of his entire career – the reproduction of the Portland vase. Found in a tomb in a sandhill at Monte del Grano, near Rome, in 1644, the vase was identified as having belonged to Alexander Severus, who was killed in A.D.235.

A Jasper reproduction of the Portland Vase, made by Wedgwood after four years of experiment. This is one of the first issue and was sold in 1793 to Thomas Hope of Amsterdam, who appears in the original list of subscribers in Thomas Byerley's notebook.

Preserved in the library of the Barberini Palace it was eventually bought by Sir William Hamilton, who sold it to the Duke of Portland. In 1786 the Duke lent it to Wedgwood who had been trying to copy it from prints, and he spent more than 4 years trying to produce a copy of the intricate and beautiful blue and white glass vase in black and white Jasper. Wedgwood was soon besieged by subscribers who wished to pay for a copy in advance. Diffident as to his ability to execute the work successfully, Wedgwood accepted orders only on the understanding that his patrons should feel free to withdraw if the finished article should fail to meet their expectations. Completed in 1789 the vase was acknowledged as a perfect copy and received the approbation of Sir Joshua Reynolds.

While Josiah senior enjoyed the applause of the connoisseurs of London, his son and his nephew undertook an extensive European tour, collecting debts and promoting Wedgwood ware in Holland and Germany, where they made a shrewd assessment of the commercial potential of the Coronation of the Emperor Leopold and ordered that special consignments of commemorative ware should be despatched to take advantage of the purses of the nobility of central Europe, gathered together for this unique occasion. Tom Wedgwood, meanwhile, was more adventurously employed in the thick of French radical politics with his friend, James Watt the younger, a 'fierce democrat'.

Wedgwood senior was now less concerned with business than with his scientific and literary pursuits. He corresponded with Lavoisier and Priestley, encouraged Dr. Darwin to promote savings clubs amongst the workmen of Shrewsbury, and was delighted at the marriage of his two sons, Josiah and John, to two sisters. He lived long enough to see a first grandchild and the courtship between his eldest daughter Susannah and Robert Darwin, son of his friend Erasmus Darwin. Falling ill in mid-December 1794, Josiah Wedgwood died on 3rd January 1795.

Conclusion

Wedgwood's career was remarkable. He can be said to have established not only a great firm but a great industry. Faujas de Saint-Fond, the French traveller, acknowledged that 'In travelling from Paris to St. Petersburg, from Amsterdam to the farthest points of Sweden, from Dunkirk to the southern extremity of France, one is served at every inn from English earthenware. The same fine article adorns the tables of Spain, Portugal and

Italy; it provides the cargoes of ships to the East Indies, the West Indies and the American Continent.'

The secret of his success did not lie, as many historians have claimed, in any technical supremacy that his discoveries—green glaze, creamware, Jasper—might have won for him, or in the skill with which he organized the layout of his factory. His inventions were quickly copied and his rivals were not slow to adopt the steam-engine or imitate his division of labour. Half a dozen historians have claimed that his managerial efficiency, his avoidance of waste and breakages, his use of cheap transport by turnpike and canal, enabled him to undercut his competitors. This apparently reasonable argument ignores the fact that his rivals were equally free to use canals and turnpikes and, unlike him, did not spend vast sums on experiments and fees to prominent artists. The plain fact is that Josiah Wedgwood regularly sold his goods at double the normal price, frequently at treble. He knew the value of quality wedded to fashion and he charged the nobility what he knew they would pay. Thereafter it was simple to sell the common people what he had made them want.

He was, in Gladstone's words, 'the greatest man who ever, in any age or country, applied himself to the important work of uniting art with industry'. His role as a leader of popular taste is more readily acknowledged than his valuable work as an industrial chemist. Elected a Fellow of the Royal Society, the friend and confidant of such leading men of science as Priestley and Watt, he could with truth say, 'The fox hunter does not enjoy more pleasure from the chase than I do from the prosecution of my experiments.' As a man of refinement and informed opinion, as a sincere philanthropist, model employer and consummate salesman, he was a titan in an age of industrial giants.

THE PRINCIPAL EVENTS OF WEDGWOOD'S LIFE

1730	Wedgwood born

- -

1744   Wedgwood apprenticed
1745   *The '45'- Charles Edward Stuart attempts to claim the throne*

- -

1753   *British Museum founded*
1754   Partnership with Whieldon
1755   *Johnson's Dictionary*
1756   *Seven Years War begins*
1757
1758
1759   Wedgwood sets up in business at the Ivy House
1760   *George III succeeds to the throne*
1761   *Duke of Bridgewater's Worsley-Manchester canal completed*
1762   Wedgwood meets Thomas Bentley
1763   Promotes turnpike before Parliament. *Peace of Paris ends Seven Year War*
1764   Wedgwood marries
1765   Queen Charlotte's tea-service
1766   Treasurer of Trent and Mersey canal
1767   'Potter to Her Majesty'
1768   Leg amputated
1769   Etruria opened. *Watt's first steam-engine*
1770   Trade marks first used
1771   *First cotton-spinning mill opened*
1772   Showrooms opened in Bath
1773   Catherine the Great's 'Frog' service
1774
1775   Jasper invented
1776   *Revolt of the American colonies*
1777
1778
1779
1780   Death of Thomas Bentley. *The Gordon riots*
1781
1782   Pyrometer invented
1783   Elected Fellow of the Royal Society. *End of the American War of Independence*
1784   *First mail-coach services*
1785   Irish Trade Treaty negotiations
1787   Society for the Suppression of the Slave Trade founded
1788

40

Principal events

1789	*The French Revolution*	Portland vase completed
1790		
1791		
1792		
1793	*Britain and France at war*	
1794		
1795	Wedgwood dies	

Bibliography

The Dictionary of Wedgwood; Robin Reilly and George Savage.

The Selected Letters of Josiah Wedgwood; ed. A. Finer and G. Savage; Cory, Adams and Mackay.

Wedgwood; by Wolf Mankowitz.

Sacred to the Memory of
JOSIAH WEDGWOOD, F.R.S. and S.A.
Of Etruria in this county.
Born, August 1730. Died January 3rd. 1795.
Who converted a rude and inconsiderable
Manufactory into an elegant Art and
An important part of National Commerce.

The monument by the artist John Flaxman RA in the chancel of Stoke parish church.

41

APPENDIX

The manufacture of pottery

Pottery in its broadest sense includes all forms of ceramic wares—porcelain, bone china, stoneware, earthenware, terra-cotta, and fireclay products—which are formed from clays and other minerals, and hardened by the action of fire in a potter's oven. The main differences between these various types of pottery are due to the nature and proportion of their raw ingredients, and the methods and temperatures of firing.

Clay is the most important raw material of the potter. In Britain, *ball clay* (which is extremely plastic and is therefore easily shaped) and *china clay* (which is essential to china) are found in great quantities in Dorset, Devon and Cornwall. *Fireclays*, which are used in the manufacture of sanitary fireclay wares, are found—generally in conjunction with coal measures—in Scotland and the Midlands.

Other materials employed by the potter include *flint* which gives both whiteness and hardness to the 'body', as the final mixture of clays and minerals is called; *felspar* which helps to bond the materials together; *Cornish stone,* used sometimes instead of felspar as a fluxing agent; and *bone ash* which gives translucency and toughness to English bone china. A material called *grog,* which is pulverized fired earthenware, is sometimes added to the ingredients to reduce shrinkage during firing. The body will differ according to the nature of the product. Chemical stonewares to resist heat-shock or porous filters for acids require bodies composed of special materials.

Modern English earthenware consists of china clay, Cornish stone, flint and ball clay in various proportions. The materials are all carefully prepared before being ground in water. The china clay is washed and made ready at the quarries in Cornwall; the flint is calcined or roasted to a white heat and crushed at the factory. After grinding to the fineness required, the materials are blended to correct proportions in the mixing arks until they are of the consistency of cream. After passing through fine mesh screens or sieves, and running over electric magnets to remove every particle of iron (which would cause dirty ware), this creamy mixture—called slip—is pumped into storage tanks.

Left; the mill and sliphouse at Etruria, taken about 1890.

Right; a thrower and his assistant at the Wedgwood Etruria factory in 1890.

Left; inside a bottle oven at the old Etruria factory.

When the clay piece has dried to the consistency known as 'cheese hard', it is ready for the turner, who shaves off the surplus clay. The motion of the lathe is then reversed and the turner burnishes the surface with a smooth steel tool.

The raised ornaments of Wedgwood Jasper ware are made in pitcher moulds, reproduced from eighteenth century originals. The clay is pressed into the moulds and the figure-maker eases the figure from the mould with a spatula.

From these tanks the slip is forced into filter presses formed of sailcloth covers screwed up in flat wooden or metal frames, which remove all surplus water. The thin plastic sheets of clay which come from the filter presses are then rolled up and placed in a mincing machine, called a pugmill, in which are a series of converging blades. In this machine the clay is minced to a homogeneous mass, entirely free from pockets of air, and brought to just the right consistency for use.

The traditional methods of pottery making are based upon

Left; Thomas Lovatt, an ornamenter at the Etruria factory, decorating an edition of the Portland Vase.

the potter's wheel and the mould; but in many factories today it is no longer possible to watch the thrower transform, as by a miracle, a dumb lump of clay into a living shape. For the traditional methods have been replaced by semi- or completely automatic machines for making tea-pots, plates, cups and saucers, and dishes. These semi-automatic machines were first tried out in North Staffordshire in 1843 when they were said to be capable of making 46,800 plates a week.

Semi-automatic machines—they are known as 'jolleys' or

'jiggers'—have been described as mechanical throwers. A jolley has a revolving metal head shaped like a plant pot into which a mould for a cup or basin is put. A lump of clay is then placed inside by the operator who brings down a lever arm to which is attached a metal profile which forces the clay against the sides of the mould. The mould thus forms the outside of the article and the profile tool the inside.

Pottery articles of irregular shape cannot be produced easily by machinery. These are made by slip-casting in plaster-of-Paris moulds. Pottery figures of crinolined ladies, toby jugs and similar fancy goods are turned out by this method. First of all the modeller shapes the article to be manufactured in clay, making due allowance for shrinkage during drying and firing. From this original model a master-mould is produced which is used to run off all the working moulds needed during production. Some moulds are made in several parts which have to be fitted together with great accuracy.

Slip (liquid clay) is now poured into these working moulds which gradually absorb moisture from the slip, leaving a thin crust of clay of uniform thickness adhering to the inner surface of the mould. When this is sufficiently thick, the surplus slip is poured away and, after allowing a short period for the clay to harden a little, the mould is opened and the article is removed. Nearly all expensive pottery or porcelain figures need a considerable amount of hand-tooling after delivery from the mould. Sometimes they are built up by the addition of handmade flowers and foliage which calls for a very delicate and dexterous touch.

Some pottery needs only one firing, and after it has been glazed and allowed to dry it is placed in the oven, protected if necessary by a fireproof box called a saggar. Earthenware is fired at a temperature of between 1,150° and 1,250°C. The old type of intermittent oven was like a gigantic wine bottle which towered above the surrounding workshops and houses giving the North Staffordshire Potteries a distinctive and almost Oriental appearance. These old bottle-shaped ovens were fired by rule-of-thumb methods which could not be controlled with scientific accuracy, although extraordinarily good results were achieved with them. Modern continuous tunnel ovens are generally fired by electricity or gas, with greater thermal control and considerable fuel economy, and their use has resulted in a much cleaner and more healthy atmosphere.

The best earthenware is fired at least three times and it is not

46

decorated until after the first or biscuit firing which hardens the wares and makes them easy to handle. Underglaze decoration is done on this biscuit ware with metallic colours 'hardened-on' to remove all traces of oil, dipped in liquid glaze and fired in the glost (glaze) oven. This third firing gives the ware a hard coating of transparent glaze which shows up the colours on the biscuit beneath and is quite impermeable to liquids.

A birth in the family
   '*She sent for the midwife whilst we were howling (after making tea for us as usual in the afternoon) without so much as acquainting me with the matter Slipt upstairs just before supper, and we had not risen from the table before the joyful tidings of a safe delivery and all well was brought to us, and as soon as the young visitor was dressed she joined the company in the dining room. The mother eat her supper, went to sleep, and all are in a very fine way this morning, but from a sort of decorum established amongst the sex, originally intended, no doubt, to impose upon us poor men, and make us believe what sufferings they underwent for us and our bantlings, I believe she does not come down to dinner today, but I shall endeavour to persuade her that the farce will no longer pass upon us in this enlightened age, and as for the mere etiquette it is not worth preserving.*'

from a letter by Wedgwood

INDEX

Figures in italic refer to the page numbers of the illustrations.